Reports

Reports

by
Wong
May

Harcourt Brace Jovanovich, Inc., New York

First edition
I S B N 0–15–176850–1
Library of Congress Catalog Card Number: 72–75419
Printed in the United States of America
B C D E

"Landscape" and "Waiting for God"
originally appeared in *Poetry;* "Report,"
in *The American Scholar* (as "Report I").

To My Mother

Contents

II

III

This book was started in winter 1968, New York,
completed September 1971, Winnipeg.

I

Christ, sever me not from Thy sweetness

—Song of the mad king Sweeney

First

I will know you by the season's first

Spring:
A body of water

The season's first
Gushes forward

Knowing no other world than this one
No other act

But the steps she will retrace
In nature, she will. No other way
Not to love

Persephone
To follow the bent of nature to the full –

The sweep of the tree downwards to reach the earth!
She will follow you into there also

Take the plunge
Her madness

She takes with her, the dogs at her heels
& a flute

Never to know night or the full weight of winter
But as a dead bird flying inward

Persephone
The whole world is going underground with you

The season's first
The season's last sundry colours

Never to know hell
But man as the climate
Woman as the country, as surely
Rules over as ruled under

As yet she knows no way not to love

Never to know hell but herself
As underground water. The despair!

Of coming forth in spring
As spring
Virgin

A body of water

November Notebook

The rain is characterized by mud.
The rain is characterized by the mud it makes.

The sky is characterized by its inability to be.
                The sky is not there.
In rage it tears everything into bits.

A stone is characterized by the speed it falls?
No. A stone is characterized by the speed it grows.

A hand is incomplete.

A knee is characterized by its unity.

A kidney disbelieves.

The face may be true after all.
The face may be the only truth.
     There is nothing behind it.

Let it be said after all
    that I want a beautiful face.

An expression is a glass
  of water. A glass of water for you.
    So I am given expression.

A voice disturbs.

The dark is characterized by what it sees.
    The owl's eye also belongs to the cat family.

A knife is characterized by what it meets.
             Guide   me.

A comb is characterized by its teeth.
   A toothless comb has much to say about us.

A hard-boiled egg is characterized by the difference it feels.
It will tell nobody.

Salt is characterized by what, sugar by what
Tell   me.

November is characterized by flayed raccoons
who go about their business in the dark
like newborn babies.

The moon is characterized by its inability to kill.
The moon is filtered.
Its death-rays reach us but gently.

A man is characterized
by his ability to

What?
To sit still. A man is characterized

by his inability to
What?

To sit still.

A spoon is characterized by the time
it spent with you.
Devils spoon-feed us.

A tree is characterized by its ability to stand
in hell.
A tree is the shortest distance between heaven
and hell?

No. The tree expresses no longing for God.

Love, I cannot walk the earth

bearing the dead weight of my body

America

What is N.Y.C. after dark

but Miss Lulu Marican
singing blues
                        her breasts pushed to her throat
                        across her body the traffic
the live wires and dead wires the neon signs
                and used tires   crossed and crisscrossed
What is Miss Lulu Marican
but a road
                to be stamped out entire

                        the universe

reduced to a scream

her soul a bowl of soup
splashed across some gentleman's white suit

She will meet you after work
                        at the corner of 50th & Broadway
the all-night drugstore

                        as agreed

Nothing will recover
                        from her singing.

                        From her silence
None
        none but America !

Business Management

                        Is that all you have to teach us

America

Silence

Silence
is wooden is a wooden horse
dead in a child's evening is at first
a short silence then
it grows

like a jaw. Silence
is the tree that follows you into your
sleep is the distance
between any two persons is
the three rocks you play with
daily

which teach you new words. Silence
is all the hooks I have swallowed
and ancient. Silence
is things to be said
quickly

and then silence.
Lend me bones, fish.
Lend me lies & distances, horizon.
Lend me nothing,

Water. Silence is the willow I throttled,
is the ghost of a swan,
is the ear I buried

the well I poisoned
all the reflections and connections. Silence
is a layer of hair and nails, all
the waste and accumulation.
Bear with me,

Beast of Burden, we
carry each other like beasts
of burden. Trying to drown
now would be

like water trying to drown itself
in water, bear with me. Silence
is the will you perfected,
the car you polished

till it shines
like a black patent leather shoe,
is visceral convulsion, is
where you sit in the owl's eye,
is all the

colors I absorb, is
5000 years of
moonlight and
fatigue

In Memoriam

(Martin Luther King, Spring 1968)

And if you come to my party
I will come to yours

There will always be parties
and poetry

Evening comes soft and grey like
a gracious hostess

somewhere she dances
for St. John the Baptist
his head

Listen: I am not sick
You are not sick

the in-patients are indoors
the out-patients are outdoors

the world is not sick

After a few martinis
people with glasses in their hands
touch each other
imagine blood

Spring is here
in April
as always

Assassins spring up everywhere like prophets

Donations
Donations

What is the occasion?
Did someone drive into the cows?

Some white men
imagine they are in Africa.

Listen
if you listen carefully for long you will hear nothing

they want peace

it's catkins falling off willow trees

Going (1)

Going into the dark may mean
going further
into the dark, not

out of it (ever), nor
really any further,
but darker. And the
gods know it: the risk
is that there's
no risk.

Send a man into
the dark, let
him investigate.
See where the
evidence of life
will finally lead him
to. And he
knows it. He says,
Remember the stars –

Heaven has such holes,
or is it the dark,
the dark too has such
holes?

He's amused.
The stars too oscillate,
though the choice is
hardly between anything.

The Wind

the wind pulls the mud pulls one
dead horse rises
from the mire pulling
another

yet another

Lord, the night is not complete

the eye sinks the feet sink
the worms bubble up

with a child's voice a child's claws
the world retreats

to the pond's edge to the pond
where the soldier wearing a string
of his brother's ears
contemplates the world

Lord, the prairie wind begs the wolf
        the wolf begs the prairie wind

all night for one small sign

where the sky is torn
Lord, indicate
the world is not complete

as the three blind mice
scuttle across the pond's floor
releasing

a fart of stars

Lord, look to the pond
where the world is reflected

Lord, look
the horror is not complete

East Bengal

Children die
Children go
first everywhere
Children are ancient
like milk
they don't keep
they are wise
like dried fish
they lie by the roadside
After Cholera
and War
they expect to see God
meanwhile
they wait
for cremation
Cholera was nice
her sari
a triple hoop
of flame she was gorgeous
Our Lady of the Rock
attended by a psalm of flies
War was nice
like Shiva
She has many arms
one face & many legs
when she dances
She is a dancer with no feet
Vultures are nice
they can't wait
they are angels
but people are stupid
they ought to get wood
enough wood
to make a pyre for all their children
meanwhile they fight Cholera
& each other
when we wait

like bottles
in Death's factory
& God is hand-woven
pressing his face close to me
a piece of cloth

Letter from the Smokehouse

Those who feed on rat's milk weep
their faces blind
their teeth grown
inward their bellies extend
like blown glass, I will be there
before you

O my darlings

Those who feed on wolf's
milk are sons of women who
tear their guts out at
the sight of their young finding
them human

O my darlings

The lion's cubs
will not sleep, in dream
they continue to see

God who bears a face
much like

theirs
Those who feed on the dead
could not fight the stench
their own those who go on

living
weep their dead blind
weep the wolves blind weep the lion
blind weep
their hunger blind weep
their gangrene blind

My pilgrims
lining up like fish
in the smokehouse, I was there before
each one of you

rotting stinking blind

the Lord of War has two jewel eyes
both have been stolen

they sit in a glass case
in the American National Museum

O my darlings

Choice Involved Madame B.

I do not know what kind of insect you are,
but you are. When I hate you enough

to want to kill you, you are
not. You evaporate into a distant

aunt (mostly sad), with 2 long front teeth
in French perfume. It is likely

that one day I will be like you?
Why, if I hate you enough, and

Why not
before thirty I will be a dead cow.

Freak Show at the Red River Exhibition

(June 71, Winnipeg)

Where the layers of flesh overlap, one sees the death of the world's most ancient lake. The tremor that passes to one from the white kerchief over his genitals is of a flesh which has long come to rest – in its own cataclysmic spread. Each fold marks the retreat of a human form, as on lake shores, the repeatedly abandoned. That the whole of his belly would ripple when there is a breeze, I do not doubt. Where does one go from here? If the breeze, in passing, awakens the world's most ancient feeling – the desolation of flesh, it is because so far inland one no longer looks back nor ahead; so far it has smacked of the circus. My sorrow that he has murdered all the lakes in the world for me once and for-ever, I pay him homage. I think of my father the bankrupt whose person knows no bounds, who through the years continues to blackmail me from heaven, I pause over such an extent of flesh, its repercussions and far-reaching effects. I pass by with my own flesh in flight, recalling only the dis-advantage of his strangely human head and his strangely foreshortened arms and legs. As one ripple extends and dies into another, the final circle finally encompasses the whole, so the flesh is spilled, spilled all over, the blue needle-marks on his belly exercise no control. As through centuries all over the world the flesh has been spilled, with no bloodshed, while they sell tickets at 35¢ per head outside the van for people to mill round his mobile home, looking in from all directions this tremendous map of a man watching TV

(bespectacled, with a writing pad under his chin and a ball-point pen in his left hand, he has the expression of a family man about 46, relaxing in the comfort of his own home at the end of a summer day)

One is seized with the desire to cover him with one's national flag.

Drawn

Drawn
like the day-lilies
                    to the sun
their throats flung open
                    inside out —

Some such small birds
            could have swallowed a tiger
drunk hot blood
            thrown up their own entrails.

The fiery red spots
they bear
            say everything
there is to be said
            under the sun. The height they
yearn to
            with their whole being drawn
forward
            emptied. Such the
nature of their passion
                    they are dangerous

they endanger
only themselves

Terra

The mineral that nudges me
is an angel

that I may know terror
intimately

I name him man.

I am porous with eyes
that I may dream him

his breath grows uneven
        grows deadly

I am loosened with air.
The angel sees

with my terrible eyes
that there may be life here

I am the suspect.
As each time
a man is found

in all things killed
all things not killed
I am the suspect.

I am guilty of harbouring
life, supporting
the unlikely

you will always find me here.

The mineral that pierces
my sides

says each time afresh
here, here, here

here also
there is a man

who has perhaps shrunken
to the size
of a stone

or is no bigger than a worm's
head

a voice crawls out :

In all things dead
and not dead

I wish to find you.

God at Six O'Clock

Check this list
    against that list

        Check this clock
           against that clock

                Check this clerk
                  against that clerk

You may also check this sunset against God
If it looks suicidal

it's possible
he thought then there is no reason why not

Muse

A fox eats himself out.

For twenty years he has lived in me

like something I have swallowed whole –

buried alive
in me.

At last I am wearing out.

Each day I throw him some meat
now at places the bones appear. What transparencies !

I am not a poor provider.

The sickness that takes such delights in me
awes me

its flora and fauna
the unexpected discoveries

there is not a part of me which has not entered
the secret tapestry

but I am the chosen consumptive.

A slow fire tends my eyelids

your head has finally emerged
through my breast

The poetry of it !

My heart you hold in your hand –
a cake of soap

Song

What wood
maple/cherry/pine or the sweetest
rosewood

Out of which
            I will carve
                       the likeness
                                 of your body
across which
              strings will be strung

It is an instrument
I have in mind
                no less the man
                            I adore
Who will not live

with me.
           I will hang you up on the wall
                                to adorn
the darkness
            singing

What wood
maple/cherry/pine or the sweetest
rosewood
              Who prefers

himself Who
would have the same for me Who
stands for Death
               waiting in the darkness
                              like a door

Winter 68

"If the salt have lost his savour
wherewith shall it be salted?"

What immaculate dirt
goes into the making of this winter's

Snow

When he takes off his boots
He takes off his feet

Nothing is North
but South of his head

his cold and pointed feet pointing forever to a truer
North.

What is there left
to piss off?

His sex
the icicle of urine.

Prince of life, he will lick the whole landscape

for a little taste
a little taste in his mouth.

No it is not him not him not my denouncement of him
but the whole world is coming

after him with
or without him: his boots advance like 2 crocodiles

Moved not by love
but by the lack of love

he will claim total possession
he will want nothing

his love a lie

which is going to come true

Looking Out

In what wantonness of pain
have I come to see
myself as
the other,   you

as another,   I no longer know.
The snow struggles all day

to form a word.   They fall.
They do not fall.   The sky
said as much.   I feel

their dizziness.
I wish I had a word.
I wish I knew a word.

The cars on the parking lot:
I own them all.

They run North they run South
they run away with my blood

I wish to God
I could spare them all.

Across the street
Every man looks like you.
Every man looks unlike you.
And it is not even you that I am looking for

On Some Success

I've given at your request
the truth
        Seeing what you're
              dying to get at

is love.
        By God
it is true—
My life depends on it—

            the imposture
that sits in my heart
pumping all day
        recognizing the necessity
             of being successful

even in love

The Bride

to Baudelaire

5000 years to prepare a bride

Footsteps underground
hurrying to sapphires to strange gods

How your absence endows me

Memory, You have grown inhuman.
I have 12 senses, all knives

Like a stone I have a secret:
It is not dead. Light,

I learn to read without.
Without needs, wholly abstract,

I have grown eyes at my back,
                              acquired
6 pots of geraniums

all red – gifts
I have not wanted, knowledge
                    I despise.

I have wandered to dark places
made discoveries
I have no words for. In my absence

the dogs have grown strange,
the trees turned black, the milk
sour. My acts have given me power

I have not dreamed of
nor asked for.
                    The black lake

has nothing in it.
These bloody stones
                I bring back

Yours
These hands Yours
These jewels I wear Yours

Cool
& congealed
in the inhuman light

they crawl
like insects
round my neck

It

The dog is sick
He has nothing to do with it.
Space
        grows in his mouth
It is our world
                not his

   He moves about freely
the space
            He does not own anymore

He will finally be swallowed by it.
The dog is sick
                like a man

He is,
        cannot keep his mouth shut
cannot bite
            or bark. Dog, Dog
there's no limit
                to a man's incapacity

We are saved by it.

Iowa City 1968

Letter to my shoes my foot my shoemaker
3 roads 6 directions, Iowa River,
My neighbour's apple tree
to last week's newspapers, to Mr. Nixon, to my people
gentle people etc.

I am not tired, resigned
or even terrible. When I say
Let go
the last small terrible mountain
Let go, I mean
only myself, I mean
I am lazy

am not a soldier, will never be one.
I would be happy to watch
the "Save 10¢ per gallon" sign
whirling whirling all day
like a lollipop. Or if there is a river—
My shoes flow back behind me
and my boat.

I'll be this blue bottle.
I've only one gesture.

                    It is not in me

to fight back desire
or sleep. Let them
speak
        of my desire
to fight back
                nausea. I proclaim

things have become irresistible.
Shoes, Table, Apples, Revolving walls,
Paper, Bulldozer, Rain please proceed

It is not a monster
who's here to eat up

its own litter.
It licks my face.
Its eyes full of light. Happiness,
You have become irresistible

On the Scene

(where Sharon Tate and four others were murdered)

Houses and Cows. Some people.
Who is not in the picture?
The darkness that outlines us all

the charcoal with which we are defined
darkly

      (how else?) against each other

Darker
for a more distinct character, darker
against the world

           the sack

that tightens

Someone ought to outlive all this a little while

growing fainter

          an indistinction

a carelessness

Dream 19

In Dream 20 I heard myself relating to a friend Dream 19, but for that I would not have remembered either. If in each dream one is to make a report of the previous, then the former is the negative, the latter the processed print; this happens to be one of the very few negatives that survive the darkroom, and the act of putting it down in writing may perhaps be called Dream 21? Is the writer overly ambitious, or has the narrator gone this far only to be tedious? But the dreamer has with him only the very few dreams that survive the act of writing, he must implore the reader to bear with him. It was in Dream 20 then, I heard myself speaking excitedly of the previous (Dream 19): that of the unsuccessful anaesthesia and attempted operation. Supposedly anaesthetized, I remember going out of the room. In another room I saw a man who looked like George. George, I said. But his face was painted with all kinds of numerals and signs. I started to read those vivid numerals on his forehead, remembered having been told (elsewhere) that when they began to disappear my anaesthesia would be near complete. As it was, only some numbers disappeared. Of those that remained, I could sort out numbers from one to twenty, every one of which in a different color. I remember coming back to my room, reasoning with the surgeons who had me strapped to the operating table that I didn't see the point of this operation. It was then one of them pointed out that both of my kidneys would have to be removed, and without any further delay. My first thought was, what frightful scars I would have on my waist. I began to plead with my mother who was also nearby. At that very instant I saw that I had come to the end of the dream, the operation had been performed, it was in fact over.

Report

        With what hands
Seize the throat of lilies
the mirror strikes
        and withdraws again.

I have bad dreams.
They are not real.
No more

than the killer
you read about,
the daily reports.
They leave me dumb & cold.
I see no evil

Speak no evil. Ten
rubies stuck
in my vocal cord. They are
not for sale. What

Good could all this
do you. Would you
learn. Could it
be taught. Light

Wraps around
me. Topaz. Today
peace settles over me
like a pool. I am
the water

that seeks again
& again to recover
the same face
        the old level.
I am the killer.
        Hell
is in another world.

The Accomplice

Howling through the woods

for hours

as if you were not going

to die as if someone

ought to kill you

I fired the shot.

You could be a dog

a wolf a moose

a last unicorn

I never saw you—

If it were only to find

a place to die

I would have told you—

Drag yourself

along as if you

were a dog

a wolf

an accomplice.

How far

can you go?

I am the silence

that follows

Must You

Must you always wake me

                    like an alarm clock
invariably

     to him

him?
Your power to call him back
always

     as if after a bath,

          looking his best −

Unfair

Landscape

(watching Lucia paint)

Foxglove : Your brush, running
in & out
of the tall grass. Fox
of that half-seen purple !
(the hand shakes a little
         across the canvas)
Swifter than the green is in April,
                         More
Contagious –
         Until
the whole field is yours
                  in summer

a breathlessness. Purple
on green. Purple in
& out
of the green. Fox
half-seen

Sister of my spirits
float
as the wind floats
across the field
purple the wild grass

Twice a Day

Twice a day the sound
of mass slaughter
from my neighbour's
poultry farm
The midday rehearsal

& the evening chorus
So the day closes twice

before it closes,
Dame Emily Dickinson,
the chorus

has always been one, the voices
the voice of one bird

a giant extinct flightless bird

the same bird they kill twice each day
everywhere

So that at the close of each
I find myself

waiting

     like the last

of a string of 3 bells

The Last Round

I have a song for you—
carrying
the white road round my neck
like a silk rope
I came for you

Just when
there seems to be
no way out no road
from here
        no one
around I came
to you

This is a way out.
Would you also carry the door
with you—
(on your back?)

Everywhere you go
you enter
at the end of the road
the same white house.
This is a way in—

how it winds round

you—

This way

all sheep go

A Word

Whose hand I'm holding

               the man

is dead. I suspect

it's a dead man's hand

I'm holding, that he suspects

                      he is being suspected.

Will the owner of the hand Please

But I cannot tell

I am moved

         or moving.

               Kindness, darkness

               I wish to say the rain

               has a scent

               to the blind, a color

                  not black, not

What you fear.

For which whose hand I'm holding

Who holds my hand now

              to write

              this

              word

Fossils

In this life
we forfeit
the next

the fish disengage
in coition

in coition
realize

it is already the next life

     *

In this life
I am your love

& in the next
& the next

In each life
we forfeit
the next

I was snail
I was algae
I was fern

In each life
you are my love

the chalk-bed says
the limestone says

we will never be
man & woman

we will never be

     *

We may never meet as man
& woman
again

but at each terminal
wait for me

     *

at the source of fire the source of water
where all sources meet

in the hollow where we were
there was a man

before he was fern
before he was algae
before he was coal

Wait for another
My love

It will be me.

Francesca's Lament

Inferno V

All the sunlight I hoarded
enough for ten years

to shield me
against

this unbroken black glass dark
at the sting

of a moment all spent
the pig's blood?   O God

What meanness
to kill

with a pin's head, though my
failings be small, your hooded eye
all wise

I am the bee
in your glass jar

reminiscing
wheatfields the daisies

their sweet mustard-seed heart

Who would have believed
My love did love me

for a day, a day
enough for ten years

of wreckage, of worse

O I am not weak
nor unprepared, but it pleases God

to kill with an absurd swoop

Now the mystery begins

Epilogue

the sand escapes
to say the sea's mouth
does not swallow
the sea-wife
is a hag She is the first
of 3 generations of widows
her lovely daughters She carries
in a sack they are not
for drowning She is the sea's
blasted motor the big heart
pounding
pounding
blasphemous, O She is loud
like a travelling salesman's
fanfare She is loud
She is big enough
for everything small enough
for everything the big heart
masticates and
masticates She is weak
enough She is
strong enough
upon whom
all tides turn
all tides
return
eternal
She is weak enough
strong enough
She is nothing
She burns sand into glass
the fire escapes
to say

II

Beautiful is man and evident in the dark

—Georg Trakl

New Hampshire, September 1969

to P. H., gratefully

Suddenly it is no longer
towards a wall
I walk,   the fields stretch out
on both sides
white

like a shipwreck in heaven.
Nobody's drowning.

Stars fall

at regular intervals
to gauge the darkness.
I am conscious of all the minute dying things
and their phosphorescence.

Stars lie here

all night to look up.

There never was a road

from here. It seems possible
to go further

much further

to move on

to a further darkness

till to look at death

I look back

So that he who is always mistaken
for someone else
dies again

tonight
it is in Italy or somewhere else

the place is not important
he concluded

there is no such thing as a place at all
there is no such thing

the oleanders or olives don't make much difference
they have laid down the blue carpet

So that he might wash his feet in it
So that

it will be said
So that it will not be said

So that
he desires only acts of no consequence

It does not follow.
Nothing follows.

The hands go away the feet go away
he finds himself

tonight
it is in Italy or somewhere else

Deep in the mirror
an embryo genuflects and genuflects

Though I am no God
nor his spokesman.

(Who dies of life
dies of rat poison –

It is for rats.
So that

at a quarter to six he said
this is only for those who dare deceive themselves

I cannot hand out prescriptions
to those who daren't

My friends My friends
with all their reasons for loving and living

My friends
who do not know hunger from thirst

their faces bloated beyond
recognition.

Why am I too given these reasons
these items to stuff a duck?

We have all been given too much time

My friends My friends
who walk around like clocks without hands

When the sky bends down again
to kiss the fragile human head

let it be said
the poet's search for happiness
is concluded here.

(He has concluded
somewhere earlier

So that he might consider
other forms of life

like this brown speck
that moves is

an ant or something else —
these words are harmless

they depend
entirely
on you

Flowers for Vicky

265 pages before the end

          why must you choose to go mad

and I stay sane?

A 12-Year-Old Dog to a 12-Year-Old Man

May the eye rest
upon this jug that jug any jug

As the last thing seen.
Have we finally agreed

on something.
Item: Kettle – a metal vessel
     for boiling liquids
Item: Doorknob
Item: Umbrella

Item: What is to be the last thing seen
May the eye rest
upon this jug that jug any jug

For I cannot say what will cost me life
I will look up each word

Item: Milk – a white or yellowish liquid
    secreted by the mammary glands
    of female mammals for suckling their young

  Scissors – a cutting instrument with 2 opposing
    blades each having a looped handle
    which pivoted together in the middle so
    that they can slide over each other as
    the instrument is closed

Madness is what I will not allow myself

My life I owe to such ignorance

Things worth mentioning:

Lungs: greedy

Heart: greedy

Liver: greedy

Kidneys: greedy

Hand – that part of the human arm below the wrist
        including the palm, fingers and the thumb, used
        for grasping or gripping

Bone – any part of a piece of the hard tissue forming the
        skeleton of most full-grown vertebrate animals

Ear – the part of the human body specialized for the
        perception of sound, the corresponding part of an
        animal

Light – that which makes it possible to see

Neck – that part of man or animal joining the head to the
        body

Pulse – the beating in the arteries caused by
        the contracting of the heart

Blood – hounds

Blood

And no one ever at the last minute turned a bird

Forgive me

tho' it offends your ears and mine
this tune is still to go on for a while

May the eye rest
upon this jug that jug any jug

but this one
that one

For the ugliness of the last thing seen
is yet unsurpassable

Nothing matches what we have in mind
(as yet) we do not want to die

May the eye rest
upon this jug that jug

any jug

Hands

          that my hands
have been small
like yours
          at various stages
smaller,
          a foetus'
opening and closing
                    at various stages
decided to stay,
                to hold on to,
I give in.
          Thereafter, what must be
a succession of hands
          comes to this –
hands of an agent
                    I play myself into
like music,
          in whose hands
I am deadly –

let go

On Landing

(after Hans Christian Andersen)

"it was her voice that made
the sky acutest at its vanishing"
—Wallace Stevens

        *

The cord that ties the egg yolk to the white
slips from my shoulder

Neither Past nor Future

the voice of my human love calling
from the dead sea gulf

Neither living nor dead

the torso of a stranger
with an angel's head

& human legs

& I once thought it's for your legs that I love thee

My human love

with a wreath of sea-roses
I crown thee

I salute thee from the deep

the element
that gives me life

must henceforth
be my enemy

no life
but its opposite

And yet there shall be no death without thee

Each wave I climb turns salt each witch swears
I shall not live

Landed
I am not more than human

What I suffer thee to see: a mere girl with legs !

Each step
a knife, a double knife

the soul I achieve
a sheer burden

My mortal love
it is not the soul I love

Never for the soul

nor the body's death

Given no human speech

on the soul's treacherous ice I dance

the dead sea scrolls
must henceforth too
be beyond me

as sight is beyond touch
or hearing

with my body
your body I worship

the human form acutest at its vanishing—

I have lost my voice

War Poem

The war is an insomnia

it goes on

when I fall asleep

The Woman he Married

Happiness
Draw a circle

Between what I cannot say and what I fail to feel

Sadness
Draw a line

Yes
I am incomprehensible

the blue ashes of words and their vain endeavours
die by inches

I've never needed your protection as badly
as I need you now

the real world
you move in like a soldier

Heart
Draw a circle

the small beasts that come suckle at my breasts

each night for darkness
May they not go over

Much as they need me
Much as I need them now

They say I will not be yours
I say I will be yours

Husband you will find me
today without a finger

tomorrow without an ear-lobe
each day something new amiss.

What is it
this woman you married?

Each day you catch me
with a word

I but half-retrieved from the dark:

a limb, a feather
a birthday candle !

No guilt too small to fill up this world

Between what I cannot save and what I have left to die

I walk as if in a purple snow
of evils, evils. The heart goes over

like a dog to his
to his vomit, the heart goes over.

Lord
how it is possible

for one to have so many fathers?
They fight for one

like sickness. If you must know

there is but one man for me
in this world

He is not my lover.

All night I press close
to him wanting to shut out

the brightness, terror.

Father who will not live

save as a voice
leading to the next

world, what is this
this gift bright as a pig's liver

this clock you nailed down with 12 black numerals
to this life

To Rilke

Dream-lilacs plucked from sleep
Sea-anemones Hyacinths Iris

Torn from what
cannot be awakened
for one is awake.   Blue hands

put me back
to where I am not.
I am not sick

Nor half asleep,   like a beast
I would strike
I would pluck all creatures
from their sleep. This
you are awakened to –

A sea-sickness
on land !   With no sea

to recover from,
when wide-awake
you are sick

to death. Doctor,
how must one
not be lonely?   What

would you – even you
say is a man's capacity
for loneliness?

Merely, the time needed
for strange things
to grow familiar

and strange again?

You are the clearest day.

City Park

1

Old woman brittle and delicate as dry leaves

                 how I grow suddenly impatient

I gasp
I can't wait to be with you

          to look out

from your phlegmatic eyes

          Summer

the last will and testament

Busy brilliant summer with its swimming pool of children

           a barrowful of Godheads!

Such our ignorance

2

The Squirrel Sonata !
3 movements: head, hip and tail

you see how I do not wish
to see you
        the sonata
is an evasion.
Little brown fellow

Do not lure me to look at you

What Keats said of his nightingale
I would say of you

Look away
Look away Little Friend

Lend me an acorn
      a book to read

this morning
I am a little suspicious of life

Epithalamium

(after Bach)

I expect to see you in the hospital of the sane
where they repair clocks and continue to deceive
the insane
I expect to see you in the hospital of the sane
if the pieces of my mind
could be gathered
I would insist
I would still insist
the world
doesn't need us
we were rapturously happy for a summer
I understand in the end you have a vision of my madness
I eat songbirds. I horrify
You couldn't tell my pupils from my nipples
I want to tell you we outlive everything in the end
Madness lasts a little longer
but not too much
For 2 months I could do nothing with what you left in my hand
In November I got married
Between one Spring
          and the next I have a child – a son
and am expecting another.
The cherry tomatoes hung like lanterns in our garden
I make pickles and jam.
And you, 30 years from now
I expect to see you in the hospital of the sane
with 2 bluebells dangling from my eye-sockets
their long stems I hold in my skull

          this is the rapture, this I celebrate

Nothing lasts, darling,
Not even death

The Orange

The orange is a doorknob
I enter.
The orange has many lungs
many windows
thrown open
to one fiery bird
under its green claws
the secret of my life
is kept. Many times
I enter

        with a clock
        ticking time
        in another world

In a moment I cannot fix
I see my life.
I begin to watch the clockface
like a jealous lover.

Song

I hang on to your shoulder
like an old coat, husband

Cast off your flesh
and I will be yours

All your 209 bones
mine

That frame
my life

Protect my heart my lungs
      my liver my womb

I will bear your children

Without you I am impossible
            an invertebrate

A tortoise
with its carapace torn off

each organ exposed
to the naked eye –

Obscene!

Enough to make your teeth clatter.

Such space

We carve

What was I before

Was I crazy
Was I pretty

from what
extremity the pulley

blazes across the rail

With what do I hope to
measure what

Was it inner
or around us
the space

Was it late

One of us
could be dead long since

but do not tell me
Do not tell

In your skull

I will get lost

The stars out there

Pluck me

Renoir's Peonies

Master

who turns all things

     you touch

into woman,

So the peonies

    are loved,

      know the pleasure

of love.

The flesh

ruffled, a wine red.

Bathed in

    that diffused warmth

the place

    must be winter

      a deep room

in winter near the fireplace.

Nothing is untouched,

       not loved.

Master

who says

a woman should be desirable—

(the flesh aglow)

      She is.

A Place in Time

"No one thing can appear in 2 places
at the same time"

this being the rule
I cannot think of anything else to do.

Morning finds me here
sitting in the sun shifting my legs

I am idle. Good-for-nothing idle.
I must be the idlest person in the world

how I astonish even myself
with such idle occupation!

     A city sits on my chest. A place with nowhere to be!
     I cannot move.

Seconds tick by like dandelion fluffs.

If I could but find you
this moment in time

what would I not give
for you to see me

sitting in the sun looking idle
even happy.

All the while the mind plays with a knife

To sink into the morning
break it

like a watermelon

To find you there
that side of time

alive without me alive
that would be no small achievement.

      The quality of morning
      The quality of morning I have come

to love: to be awake
without you without you, transparent as a knife
is transparent

the sunlight that arrives
the sunlight that is simultaneously

everywhere arriving
arriving! when I cannot

even put down one foot

A shiver goes down my spine

for the seventeenth time Morning breaks on my head
for the seventeenth time today

you have violated all the major laws
of time and space. I fear for you

as I have never feared for you now
Where is there a place

in time? That you must henceforth
run for your life

      (and these be words that never get written

I hear you.
May you escape

me even as life escapes
me, even as these words must, go

out of sight, touch, hearing:

Let our senses be our despair

the clock that man invented to tell time
& Time man invented to say

when you will die

(I've but shifted one foot in time

New England

the trees grow thickest
                    where animals die
where birds & small beasts rot
                        (a sweetness
of sorts
the trees grow absolutely wild

Love, the air
is fresh

the sky an oblivion

violets are everywhere
coming

the earth always turns up
            with something to say
the earth never fails

                              O Life
that at its most lifelike
                        looks
towards Death

Song

May no harm
come to you ever. May
no harm

       all day

I sit around
         listening
insisting
that I heard
the sound. May no harm

Come to you
ever. I repeat—
        the skin
         when stretched
       will   make a drum

a sound
not unsimilar –

       May no harm

Come to you
ever. It's dull
dull
    like a needle
going through the blood
        the dull blood song

it's dull
dull loving you

I've grown superstitious

Activities of a June Day

1

As I was flying a kite
opposite the Misericordia Hospital
all the lines
slip clean out
of my palm
the love lines life lines
Fate lines

by God
it is easy
to go where
one wants to go

Fate I say
Fate I see you
on the other shore
haul in your net work

I am returning herewith my corpse

2

& the wind is like a sleeve
splashed
with wine

3

I trace under the lampshade

the advantage of a 4-chambered heart
over a 2 (fish) or
3 (amphibian) heart

4

the delicate bones
of a kite. Bat

My blind child, I trace you
out of sight

I angle in black air
Nothing rises

to my bait
but the incredible

pulse of my life

5

And the night
is a scream
cut
short

I wake to another
without sufficient anger

I love you.

Testicles

                    the right is
                    plum-colored

the left is
a blue egg & looks older than the right.
Both have no shell, are not
in danger. At rest, they dream

                    of unknown countries

in individual sleeping bags.
The weight grows
in my hand till
              my arm
              branches out for support

before I know it I am there

                    waist high in earth

I know my power

83

Rumpelstilzchen

You say I have the voice of one who is always pleading
Yes, but that I am

I am shrewder than you think
when I tell my child a story before he falls asleep

It is merchants of the dark
I am bargaining with

the sharp shrill ones. Yes I sound harsh
I am harsh

till my voice drops off
like a pin

I will not speak.

I say
let all else go

I want this one thing stand
bright as blood

that it will cost me life
You can be sure.

Listen, you may be God
Not that I care but

Only through this I care
the rest

is the morning after

New York 69

When I think of
those unloved women and their lustrelessness

their whole life an afternoon
among certain furniture

their body a cold luncheon

I think of eyes waiting like shoes
on the doorstep

I think of certain poison

& all around the sound of things
falling shut like boxes

On Arriving

Something comes between us.
I cannot see you.

> A train going South.
> A block of building.
> A table.
> The fact.

Over the years
I have placed many things between us.

> A man.
> A woman.
> Another man.
> Brick by brick

they become mine,
nearer, more human.

Tell me I owe all this to you
Tell me nothing has actually happened

If ever I were to make the leap
If ever I were

It would be to remove myself

> not this chair
> this table, this bed, my God
> I would touch nothing human

When suddenly you will find even distance is not possible
Distance bounces back
like a snapped rubber band
to your eye

Through years I came over the bridges
like a wind, like a Portuguese nun
Today I stopped.

Closer to you
than your ears are close
today I cannot remember you.

My ancestral horse
nobody understands you.

Today I am near your heart.
I am cold.
I am what you suspect

        the sum total of all the people
        you have loved

        the irreducible zero

Son & Co.

(sketch of Michelangelo's *Pietà*)

Sweet Jesus dead
or dying on her lap
What passion

What passion
as she looks down now
   as on a lover

Sweet blood Sugar
Never was Jesus more sensuous

   the flesh more desperate

As she looks down now
Sweet Jesus

What drives man crazy:
Son, you are wanted

Alive or dead

Hair

& all around rain falls like hair

To go out
To go out to which side

To which side
Where there is no rain

                    where there is
                    not this finely falling thing
                    we understand so well

What do we have What
But this madness we also shared

Tribute to J.C.

Who is to say what
is the most important thing anyway –
The most important thing used to be: You lived

You lived. A quiet man.
I could never make you say

What is important or necessary.
As often one is troubled

by the clarity of things
after rain. Each tree seems to stand

a little further apart.
Who is to say what

holds your attention
so completely   or   what   you want me

to see?

Unbearable
Unbearable

It has become clear to me.

I Share

I share with the rats my soap my candles
I share with the mosquitoes my blood my taste for blood
   my blood
I share with the ants my food my body my hatred
I share with the sparrows their daring their noises their
   droppings
I share with the lizards what lizards like

I don't understand it

       My confusion I share with you
       It is not peculiar

What do you want you want
that I do not want for myself
What do you have you have
but that which
I wish to spare you

The moon's language the lizard's language
the rat's language

My mother's language with its 62 dialects
is also pain

the way you turn
to go

Letter to the Dark

The young of a fox must needs ever be
a fox, Son of Man

as I weep over my parents
I weep over my children now

the rows of teeth in the churchyard
and their slow decay

Why should it concern me?

I watch my forehead go
each night into the dark

to touch my father, wanting to help
wanting to know the one animal
that lives on blood.

Why should I care?

The space that I am
I still cling to: my lostness
where the chromosomes dance like small bent nails

the music of the sad cosmos and its ruined stars

I am stretched upon nothing.
For twenty years some God has fixed me

with a look. Why am I here?
I am no phoenix, nor the last
prophetess

Roots of your eye teeth tongue
stir in me. Another life is due
Another devourer!

Against such likeness
I have no power

Each time I try to break out of my form
My blood flows back

the muscles of the universe contract

I wake up
wanting to vomit.

For having tried,
I am a failure.

Son
you had better be man

Song

To the stillness comes my song
as if of stone

as if of the inside
of a stone

simultaneously the moon
the echo, the innards

of a sound, as of a pitcher
filled, simultaneously
within

without, of sound
of silence, a light

unquestioned; as the movement
of wind over a wheatfield

long gone
long passed by, simultaneously
the shoulder

the forehead, the luminous wrist,
simultaneously from all sides

seen, heard; a humming
as of bees, simultaneously
the shore

the desire
to go over, to pause, simultaneously the end

as foreseen; the grace
withheld forever

from the tongue, the pores, the hair,
love of the flesh

held for a moment in the stretched
dewdrop

the life herein.

Spare us.

Presence

One peony suffices.

One single white peony
upon which
the whole room
revolves

     is riveted

And so I thought I have come to be

No not white
there never is

but white as each
petal reflects
all light

     rejects all

the white itself
deceives

As the brain in the skull
is thought

     to be white, or so
     the white blooms

is a bloom,
the perfect disease.

Deceive me.

Bird Song

Variations

1

After the honeysuckles
the rosehips, the cherries, the honeysuckle berries

Summer sits on the fence
knitting thorns
thorns and berries

Her heart
a bird's
Wild
bird's
My little mother

All night you knit

the wild joy of thorns
and berries

A sheen of blood over all fruit
My mother

2

Rosehips, cherries, honeysuckle berries
Who would have guessed

from those brief blooms they come

into summer? After the hawthorn
the chokecherries, blueberries
hawthorn berries, in the leaves

a million
eyes of blood
watch me. However I come

into these woods I come
the most wanted murderer.

Red cells, white cells, till nothing
in my nature is not disintegrated

is more pointedly
alone.   There.

Night Letter: June

A second storm
on the heels of the first

Big sister

A bird stands on your shoulder
before your shoulder explodes

And overnight
everywhere

the toes of mushrooms

5 Disjointed Pieces

1

As the last button on my winter coat
is not exactly a friend

he knows me well
enough to be my enemy

So I wait for no final joy
nor misery, playing with

this bit of thread like a dentist
I await for nothing to transform me.

2

Where the field ends
the sheep fall

So all my creatures have turned to stone

the year ends sharply
with no scent, nothing

from the sage, the scrub-pine,
the sarcophagus

to say how the season ends

but the decomposition of foot & foot, the mouth
that burns black in my palm

is a poppy, already it is a word
that belongs to the dictionary.

3

Where the field ends
I set off

An eggcup to balance my head against calamity

And so we are cheated
of both the joy

and the final misery

knowing no more than God
the Jew that He is:

We are spared nothing

4

Here I sit
an old man in the sun

2 bones for the duchess
2 stones for the kidney

My eye an oyster

An old man
the color of shoes

5

When I think of your mastery and mine
I begin to understand how this poem

is warped
is as I have found it

warped. Let me be true

at least to where it went wrong.

Re:

"When the black and mortal blood of man
has fallen to the ground before his feet,
who then can sing to call it back again?"
—The Agamemnon Chorus—Aeschylus

Reverse death
Reverse dying
That the cups may again be filled
Fruits heaped on the table

Blood run in the veins

Bird of ashes
Horse of torn limbs
Reverse the dream

Return to claim
the long lost
            the unheard of
the barely recognizable

human face.
I will not fill your mouth
with sand your ear with rocks

Reverse the madness
the echo of the scream
That the dull stain
on each of these four blind walls
May return to his hand
He who has long since forgotten to kill
May he also return

                ascend to hell

Remembering nothing

of this language

November 1969

The half arc described by the black crow
is but a moment of your time, Italy

Night's ankle for a moment
caught in your hand

the transit daily passes into the eternal

One must imagine
Time stands still for a while here

Day
and Night stop

in the circle
of their eternal mad run

the hills step forward

the shadows descend
the olive groves a mist

inviting a plunge

I am but a thought to cross your mind, Italy

the black crow describes
in so many half arcs

to the end
the sky shall be an exile from earth
the day an exile from night

the run must of necessity
be endless

if ever one should come to doubt
how eternity spends its time

Dawn

Dawn
I want more Night
I want more Darkness
I want more more
of earth of sun
of you and if it is dark
Darkness I want more. Earth
I want more more
of you of your beasts
your creatures your ferocious
root-plants your birds
of prey of the world, of everything
that makes me poor.
Poverty
I want more more
of you more
of my thirst
my hunger
Make me love
my thirst and my hunger
they are my own

Lord

Permit me to
want more

More of your pleasure more
of your displeasure
your lies

your truth
your fire your air your water
of everything on earth and if they are bad
Bad, I want more

On Turning

But I could not ask anything to bear with me
this furniture too is separate

these hands

I could not bid the small moon to die for you
perhaps I would not

I sit looking at the cupboard, the table, my hands
as if my look could change the world.

Why should I give them pain?
I love them.

If from these dumb things I demand speech
it is no more than what I would ask of myself

for days
I cannot bear to hear myself speak

I discover perhaps
the glue

is all there is
the glue that persists

at the back of the eyes

Somehow I sit polishing
eternity and its nine black rocks

If from any of these ventures I could save
a sesame seed

I would call it
My love

I would call anything
My love

Speak to me.
Until you speak to me

I cannot write.
Approaching poetry, the unhoped for

the never to be hoped for
turning

I have lost my speech.
Approaching speech

I have almost lost my life.

Speak to me

The Heart

The heart longs
to go behind the tall grass the daisies
the yellow white blue tangled
wild things like a child
going behind them

to piss
The heart longs
to go behind this day this hour this sunlight
for an hour ten days before

or ten years from now Cup my face
in your hands Tell me I was silly
to grieve Tell me I was silly
to not grieve

To My Mother

Does the hair feel pain
Do the fingernails complain

All right pain
is what connects me to myself
but your pain is yours

It separates us
as it goes on I realize
perhaps it only means to prepare us
each separately
for death

All right
Prepare us
May you at last occur to me

as a glass of water by my bedside
Yes we have loved

How much of you has failed
to reach me

Would someone judge by that
you have failed

I observe each day again
perhaps I cannot help you

How much of you is only pain
Please step forward

But already I understand less and less
I can separate nothing from nothing

Beginning September
I should be expecting your cancer report
which I will never get

I remember
as a child I began to be aware of language
only when I began to be aware

painfully
how I cannot write without a pen

about you
Yes, even about you

I will perhaps never write about you

to this day I consistently write about other things

I wish so often love were otherwise

I wish so often to completely enter

the bark
the stone

to part-take
a scheme
so vast, so minutely hopeless

perhaps one does not even have to call it love

I go on

Canto XXXIII

The fire that the fire sieves
the water
the water sieves

wrung from the ropes of sand
the water

secretes a name
I alone decipher
as song

the fire sieves the water sieves
salt falls through the air
O Brightness of Brightness

Where
everywhere the wound calls
the echo
the wound

I am the last stitch of the needle
I am the throat
Whose jugular vein
Sings like a wire

Do not die
but the fire also keeps its promise
in each circle

in each circle
I bid you

Do not die
My voice will have nothing to travel
upon

Nothing enables me to say
anything

I am nothing I have hoped but the fire

the fire runs to meet
in each circle

from circle to circle and hand in hand
the fire on rat's feet

is also futile.
Do not die
but have we started already

My face two blind holes to reach you
even then so briskly
I have imagined

the water
in the mire, the water
out of the mire

the shade that passes through the fire
light as a shuttle as a fish

this is perhaps not the water's wish
nothing is as we have imagined

sweet verse
forged sweetly link by link

the fire also has no voice
whatever

but where you are
I leave footsteps unlike mine
where I am

the fire sharpened to a glad light

I sometimes wonder if I am alone if I may presume

the cat's dribble down
the face of universe I alone
read
as signs

If I may jot this down quickly

the fire heals the water heals the dark
illumines

at all points
the dark illumines

by whose light
I read you

the fire's prayer the fire repents
the water's prayer
the water
laments

to the last dissolves incompletely
the blood, the bone, the ligature

the fire behind
the fire behind the fire
the horse-faced rose

is my love the wheel

III

Blessings

The Divine Comedy

So each man labours on his divine comedy. That Dante has 34 cantos in the first part and 33 each in Purgatorio and Paradiso, and thus makes both fall short of Inferno by one canto is perhaps neither an accident nor, as the scholars have hoped, part of the scheme. I have dreamed of a book with 33 cantos in each section, but in the course of writing I find the first part interminable, the second the same duration, the difference being poems of the first seem to multiply by themselves, while the second is one long stagnation. How I arrived at the last part, I was not given the grace to remember. This much I know: it is not until then that I begin to see the whole "procedure" as that of the divine comedy. That my Paradiso must fall short of both, 15 by Inferno and 19 by Purgatorio I deduct by simple mathematics. But in re-reading the whole, I find my vision of Paradise gets increasingly complicated, so that many of the poems which I thought should go in the first actually belong to the last. Conversely, some nights I woke up in panic thinking the book didn't really fall into any parts, but belonged to a fearful whole—that it was the first or the second which comprised all. Nevertheless, one must attempt at some kind of division, since, God only knows, this may be the whole point of the comedy.

For Love

To allow waste:
Miles of green fields

for no purpose. For no purpose
the sky itself, a stretch of time

the infinite ! Here at last
one breathes again. To have enough

Always,
Never to run out of : as if
no place were barren enough!

Not to make room for love
but to have it: to allow waste

Waste of love
or life itself –

For we cannot otherwise
afford it.

Spring 1971, Canada

What do the birds know

but the birds are North again

in 5000 B.C. as in 2000 A.D. –
                       One must imagine a call
Each day brings fresh arrivals
the blue birds the wild geese the thrushes the crows
Each within its appointed time
                       One must imagine a King of the North
playing his ancient lyre
                       in perpetual winter
Remembering the mates he has lost.

One must imagine him immortal.
Each chord he plucks
                  draws the bird and its lot
nearer North. His lone voice
speaks of Spring,
mating, migration, the inexplicable
laws. He promises
nothing, but sings
only of those who perish on the way

Nothing brings the birds

more surely

home. One must imagine him human

and irresistible

May

The drowned dead arise

dripping wet: the look of water
asserts itself on earth, in May

the form of a tree
the Weeping Birch!

I should have guessed.
Each time I walked by
Your green tassles touched me

I felt half-dead. When and in what
previous world had we lived

and were found dead together
How far had we since travelled –

That I should find you here
on earth
             setting your foot
on earth

No doubt you recognize me

             I cling to
My brown paper bag of groceries
as if any of those things

could save me from Hell the whisper
of Hell in my ear

Since when have I stopped mourning
for you, Why am I cold?

Of this World

Of all the worlds this is the most complete:
the enchanted

Of a distance entirely made
of rain

A silence entirely
rain-filled

Among trees the rain
weaves its own leaves, repairs
with sounds its tiny imperfections, repairs
my ears my eyes
attunes me

to the movement
of snails of toadstools of roots of hairs

to the impassable greater distance

A circle
formed entirely
of wolves –

it is magic.

Where the lions too
stand fascinated

as if we were dancers
at the center

enthralling all spheres
all Gods and beasts
with human blunders

our grossly imprecise
gestures.

Towards the furthest circumference –

I am a bird
charmed by the smell of bread

drifting from the chimney of the Belgium Pastry Shop
each evening at six

the magic from which

I cannot tear myself, of all the poets

I am the most devoted, side-tracked
only by a desire to err, I am the most entirely
of this world

May: Last Day

I sit forgetful

peeling the lilac stem

till the whole stem
evolves wet green naked

cold against my flesh
                    lurid
like a snake or a saint
disappears

into my left nostril

What does a man know of lilacs?
I have not wanted to get at
the secret of their life.

I shock myself beyond words.

Thoughts of the Body

1

Thoughts of the body audible as aquatic plants

As Dawn milks his cows outside my window

Thoughts of Buddha come to me

Thoughts that shape the lines of the body

like the folds of skin on the body

of Buddha

Yes I am glad that I am mortal

I am jealous of nobody

Tell Krishna Tell Shiva not to be jealous of me

2

Dawn's blue bottles

I collect on my way

Someone from under the bridge

Calls me

Yes we are all a little jealous of our body at times

Something in us wants terribly to die

with our body

3

I knock out 3 of my front teeth

4

I take my body across the street

I take my body up 3 flights

I take my body thru the door

My body and I cross the street
My body and I go thru the wall
My body and I fall asleep
My body and I sit up

In his dream I am a pig
In my dream he is pig
        half in and out of sleep
I stumble into my body

I see myself half in and out of the door
        lengthwise on a crosscut saw

I tell my body
I'm not sure I love you any more

I have my body
My body cannot hold me at all

I see my life suspended on a thread
I grow giddy—
Why should you be attached to me?

I steal out of my body like light
from a house

I rob myself

My body I said
To what level shall I raise you

                (the great love you bore me

O sulfur dioxide

Yes I agree it is kind of silly

5

I will corrupt you even from under here

Under these acres of butterflies

you won't find me

Going (2)

The rose is a process!

the curved lids of the rose
as the eye follows
the rose becomes endless

          infinite
        as the eye goes

       each instant anew

the rose is no escape
        no end of !

The eye continues

For the rose within
the rose within the rose
        in search of

a rose, the eye
in near extinction goes

      beyond each fixed instant
beyond what the eye can see

The rose has seen you

August 71

The man who spends half a day eating and half a day nursing his nausea discovers there is not a thing in this world that he would do which he would rather not do. Every act involves a desire for its opposite, every wish or intent calls up a wish for the other, at the root of every taste the teeth sit wanting, the teeth sit wanting to bite into the tongue, the teeth who would rather not, the tongue who wishes to retract the taste, the tongue who would rather not. The man thus achieves a spontaneous simultaneity. One day, half-crouching – a posture which is simultaneously standing and sitting – he discovers a blue flower at his elbow. It seems unnatural, but under such circumstances there is nothing more natural than to watch it – breathing, as it were. Whereupon, the world becoming conscious of the man and his absorption in the plant declares him mad. The man is literally breathing with the plant. Some prefer to call it sleep. At which point the man learns newly – he is cured; also, to the end of his life he will remain devoted and lonely.

On Turning

The crab apple that I pressed to my mouth
burst

and I was bitten.
Not even the sun could bite harder

nor a saint could bite half so hard
nor my mother

On turning, even the wind takes flesh,
becomes a desired shoulder.

Of those people who have sunk their teeth into me
their tongue touches my voice

I sing.

These poems I spit out like God's
blue teeth

St. Paul I — Corinthians 13

Let me for once say what I wish to say
with grace

Hold my head

Though I speak with the tongue of men and of angels
I am nothing

Though I give my body to be burned
I am nothing

I am nothing if I were mad

I sing of the sun
the source book of objects

Let this morning come back after 2000 years
                                    with its cups of coffee

May what I see be with you without my eyes

I sing of the white rattan chair

I sing of the light that finds me here

I sing of my felicity

In the sun the white rattan chair is transfigured

An object gone crazy with the pull of the sky!

Winter Solstice.

The light darts off in 1662 directions at once
                                    like water like horses

as if on an assassin they fall—

a chorus of the deaf, the wholly incredible!

I see a bundle of more than casual lines
                        bound together by more than casual cause

So that what I want to say is almost visible

Thrown into that pit of light

Saul

as St.-Exupéry says
I see now "Love is not looking into each other's eyes

but looking in the same direction

The White Stone Horse

The white stone horse wants to die.
The white stone horse has no words to express mistakes
   or errors.
The white stone horse finds the world incomprehensible.
He looks out of his eyes into a stone interior out of it
into another.
There is nothing he does not understand except mistakes.
The white stone horse is continually surprised.
If he could but put everything into words
the world would vanish, people would vanish
old men and women, boys and girls and housewives
with their cartful of mistakes.
But the white stone horse cannot imagine mistakes.
He is made of a pile of stones with 3 black roses.
A rose for each of his eyes.
The third rose
He tears at daily. He does not understand it.
The third rose. Does he suspect that it could also be a
   mistake?
He could tell nobody.
He dreams of a language so perfect that half of the
world and its people would vanish
when correctly expressed through his language.
He dreamed of it word by word, sentence by sentence.
But first of all, he has to dream of the mistakes.

To imagine love for instance, one must first
imagine no less than three mistakes.

The white stone horse wants to die.

Someone Loves Me

And I was the question
the mirror

sees again
Each time it says

Suffer no pain
Remember as you were born

you were promised no death

Each time I drink from the river
        I see the garden

the tall grass the thistles I say
Is that where the Past

lives
How could it live
without me

Each time I saw the garden
I was not there

not in it
I was made to drink from another river

Halfway from
where he lives

a face
passes over my face endlessly like a cloud

pausing says:
the mirror has been shattered

the mirror has been shattered
repeatedly

into a spider's web
with you at the center
so obviously not killed.

Hurrying already I am back
from where I was

where someone loves me
where I live

once mysteriously always

the same person loves me
I live.

The Stone Steps of St. Peter's

(Summer 71, Winnipeg)

The stone steps of St. Peter's lead to the river
Where the Indians came to church

by boat in 1832.
Thistles & daisies

all the graves are overgrown

Where the Hudson's Bay Co.
erected a stone

for a Saulteaux Chief
a friend

It says
Our friend

Our friend
who walks on bones of his children's children

to heaven

So the Indians are cheated of their land
& all the buffaloes driven to the sea

the Governor General drinks tea
the diplomats & tradesmen drink coffee

the Saulteaux Chief continues to dream one dream

the rest is history

the stone steps lead to St. Peter

the land
that much a man takes up

when he lies down

thy kingdom come

thistles & daisies

The Bird

The bird is
        paradisiacal
is lost
dazed by the darkness of the room
it lights up. It is
not you.
I stroke him
feather by feather
back to place. He shows me
his claws. I hold him
in my hand like a lamp.
Do not die, I say
I scarcely believe in you
Do not not die, I say
I scarcely believe in you
Keep me alive, I say
by the light of my blood
I will paint you
feather by feather.
I did.
It was you,
labelled
the most beautiful thing that happened in my life.

Do not believe in me.
Do not not believe in me.
Love, I am a pathological liar,
Erase me
word by word
alive

Bliss

The sight of the telephone wires stretch across the blue air

this Spring morning

says everything that is precious to me

about human communication. I don't pretend to read music

but the script is in the air: Staves
of ineffable crossings. Against such a line

a sparrow may drop
dead
its head blown off with a blue spark, charged

                       with the more than human –

it is my doing. My own life I stretch

from pole to pole like this. I have never paid so much
attention

to the world as now, the world
as a sensory system

depends solely
on these tracings in the air – the vigilant

the vibrant transists!

Listen
I charge you

You schoolboy with a brown cap
how much could you bear

My life depends solely

on the living

To Dante

        Star

how you
spiral through eternity

            around a point

            throw yourself

into the night
            in utter abandonment
like a leaf

in ever widening
            diminishing
                  circles
Centripetal
    Centrifugal
        constantly risking death
Death or is it madness

Is it a loneliness you want to lose

Reckless one
how unerring
        you remain

        Star

So centered

Have you ever feared for your sanity

Waiting for God

(after Simone Weil)

In a distance he looks human
& is forever on his way

Coming nearer
he looks like a beast

In a way I'm
almost certain
that he is a beast –

he looks oddly familiar
& is forever on his way

        Coming nearer
        he looks like me

     ***

Flowering objects
Familiar animals
human forms
these I abandoned on the way
like old clothing

To have come this far
is madness
To go further
is not very far
from home. In midday
the pigs & other familiar sounds
are again audible

To have said this much
is madness
is why our history
never got written

In a distance
I look human
& am forever on my way

                ***

I am no more than an image
of myself 2000 years before
The well is a telescope
I enter endlessly

Every 200 years I happen again
I meet the same people
I will suffer the same and do the same

All that I am walks into this:
All that I have been

            God eats me up like a lotus
            God will forget to end the world

Blessings

I run cold water
to forget everything I have learned

A bird's shrill voices
say more than all the poets
through centuries

put together.
          I watch
out of the bathroom window
      the sky turns blue
            turns indigo

before getting dark.
The houses take on a
chalked look. The washing
on the clothesline dances
like apparitions.

I see my grandchildren.

Nothing is stranger
than Spring. I smell blood in the wind.
I accept the offerings

of one who died for me
in the Tang Dynasty. I do not know him.
I do not know him.